VOYAGES TO THE INLAND SEA 3

*The third of a series*
*on contemporary Midwestern poetry*

# Voyages to the Inland Sea, 3

*Essays and Poems by*

R. E. Sebenthall    Thomas McGrath    Robert Dana

John Judson, *editor*

Center for Contemporary Poetry, Murphy Library

University of Wisconsin—La Crosse, 1973

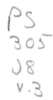 Permissions to reprint are gratefully acknowledged—

*Western Humanities Review*, 1971, for R. E. Sebenthall, 'The Artist as Hero,' *Perspective*, 1967, 'Two Nuns on a Beach,' and *Perspective*, 1968, 'Under the Volcano.' All poems also in her book *Acquainted with a Chance of Bobcats*, Rutgers University Press, 1969.

*The Movie at the End of the World*, 1972, Swallow Press, for Thomas McGrath, 'In the Hills of Wyoming,' 'The Buffalo Coat' 'The News Around Midnight,' 'Poem,' and 'Used Up.'

*The Power of the Visible*, 1971, Swallow Press, for Robert Dana, sections 12, 13, and 16.

# CONTENTS

## THE COUNTERCULTURE AND POETRY

### 1

THOREAU once said that there was no more Herculean task than to think a thought about this life and get it expressed. Elsewhere he called the intellect "a cleaver; it discerns and rifts its way into the secret of things."

With this for text, I would like to begin dangerously by saying that I believe the most important basic elements of a poem are its intellectual content and structure. Without these—without a dialectic, if you wish—to serve as backbone the poem sprawls and falls, goes nowhere. The finest imagery, and metaphor, the richest sensory detail, cannot save the spineless poem, cannot give it the strength and toughness, the concision, tension, and irony that characterize the best poetry. Yeats learned this in middle age and as a result went on to become one of the giants of the twentieth century. If he had not learned it he would have ended as he began: a minor poet. His has, of course, become the classic case for the point I wish to make here.

I know this is not a season in which to say a good word for the intellect as a valuable instrument in the making of poems. The counterculture has hustled the mind into exile with the same fanatical zeal that led earlier puritanic generations to hustle the flesh into exile. The flesh once bore the blame for all that was wrong with man and his world; now it is the mind's turn. Don't think: feel . . . Don't structure: fragmentize . . . Don't build: raze . . . Don't reason: hallucinate . . .

All this represents an understandable revolt against the often barren ends—technology, materialism, systematism—toward which much of man's intellectual effort has been directed. And, unless we are naive enough to suppose the counterculture represents the ultimate pinnacle of man's achievement, a finality beyond change, we can be certain that the pendulum will swing back, probably to another equally unfortunate extreme as pendulums have a way of doing. Meanwhile, for our time at least, thinking has become something of a dirty word and salvation rests in a return to various forms of superstition and primitivism: astrology, I Ching, tarot, neo-Fundamentalism, the vocabulary of "wow" and "groovy" and "you know." That all this amounts tacitly—and often explicitly—to a devaluation of the intellect seems obvious; and these notes propose to take a look at how this devaluation of the intellect relates to today's—and perhaps more importantly, tomorrow's—poetry. For it is the young poet now drinking at these dubious wells who will speak to the next few generations.

R. E. Sebenthall

When Gary Snyder says: "A Mind Poet / stays in the house. / The house is empty / And it has no walls" we do get an impression that Mind Poets are a very dull and restricted breed. Yet we may fairly ask: what precisely does he mean by a Mind Poet? A poet who believes that intellectual content is a legitimate and valuable element of poetry? Who precisely would he characterize as a Mind Poet? Donne, Eliot, Stevens, Yeats, Pound, Moore?—men and women who brought intellect as well as feeling and imagination to their work? Or is he speaking of the dry-as-dust pendants and cerebralists who periodically enjoy some vogue but never in any case outlast their time? These are highly important questions. But Snyder does not enlighten us. All he really succeeds in doing is planting "mind" as a pejorative word in the heads of thousands of young poets too callow and naive to examine the statement in depth or weigh its implications.

One puzzling aspect of all this is the fact that a good many of the poets who are preaching anti-intellectualism

to the young are themselves men of considerable intellectual accomplishment and their own poetry seldom reflects
the kind of mindlessness they seem to be advocating. One
wonders if they understand what they are doing, how lit-
erally they are being taken by the young who have little
judgment with which to handle a dangerous message. It
is one thing to be told to let the wind sweep the mental
rubbish out of one's head when one's head is packed with
a vast accumulation of knowledge and experience, some
of it undeniably useless. But the heads of the young are
seldom that well-packed, and to them the term "mental
rubbish" can easily begin to include the equipment for
even the most rudimentary thinking and reasoning.

Dwight MacDonald in *Against the American Dream*
has spoken of "the combination, usual only in writers of
the first rank, of acute sensuousness with broad philosophical themes." Whatever one's hopes or pretension
concerning rank, this seems to me a most desirable working "combination" for a poet. In one sense the poet has
no subject but himself, and his ideas—his philosophic
position, if you will—are as much a part of his poetic personality as are his emotions concerning a love affair or
his sensual response to a bite of fruit. But if he has no
ideas—beyond the idea of rejecting ideas—he has thrown
away, or failed to acquire, half his working equipment.
To take only one example, the acute sensuousness we
find in Wallace Stevens's *Sunday Morning* would be nothing without the underlying philosophical theme. The poem
could not in fact exist without this intellectual structure,
since every line, every image, every verbal felicity of the
poem flowed from the poet's complex mental and emotional reaction to the idea of a world without God.

The poet, it seems to me then, has two reservoirs on
which to draw for his work—the sensory and the intellectual. Neither can be too well-stocked; and one without the
other is virtually useless. A young poet will generally have
little trouble stocking his sensory reservoir. But he can-

not deal with broad philosophical themes if he does not have a well-stocked intellect. The young poet who makes a fetish of rejecting the past, who has little or no knowledge of history, anthropology and philosophy, who has not read widely in the poetry of the past, lacks all perspective. He cannot sharpen his technique if he has no knowledge of prosody. If he has no knowledge of the voices and styles in which other poets have spoken he cannot develop an individual voice or style; he cannot know whether he is working with fresh insights and fresh language or merely reiterating what others have said and probably said in a more effective way. He is confined to his own small particular point in time and space; he shares the child's inability to look at life—and himself—objectively. He lacks the indispensable tool for relating—as the best poets do—the particular and the universal, for creating—as the best poets do—a whole and rounded world.

*R. E. Sebenthall*

13

It is he, in short, who "stays in the house" and whose "house is empty."

2

It has always been tempting to claim that poetry once meant more to ordinary people than it does today. But it has never been true. The ancient sagas and legends held men enthralled only because they were tales of battle and heroic exploits. Elizabethan theater attracted the common man for much the same reason: he enjoyed the story and the action; the poetry went right over his head. During the Victorian era poetry enjoyed considerable popularity because it voiced the pious platitudes and saccharine sentimentalities that many people could understand and approve. In short, poetry becomes palatable to the public at large only when it is made a vehicle for stories or—as Rod McKuehn has demonstrated for our day— a vehicle for sentimental banalities.

Nevertheless, many of today's young poets are again laboring under the delusion that poetry can be "returned to the people." They talk of a poetry that "speaks to our time" and cite the popularity of coffeehouse readings, rock and folksong concerts as evidence of a poetic renaissance.

But several things must be noted about all this. First, the best poetry is always timeless; it speaks not merely to the poet's time but to all time. No harm in choosing to speak to one's own time if one understands and acknowledges the inherent limitations of the product, if inflated claims are not made for it. Secondly, if "returning poetry to the people" involves stripping it of the intellectual subtleties that might baffle the high school dropout and employing the idiom of a common speech which presumably makes it readily accessible to the dullest and least attentive audience, then it is a debased and ersatz product that has been returned to the people—a pop poetry, if you will, but nothing more. Again, no harm in a pop poetry if a distinction is perceived and acknowledged as, say, the difference between pop and classical music is perceived and acknowledged. But when it comes to poetry the distinction tends to be lost; and young poets are encouraged to regard a debased and ersatz product as the Real Thing —the pinnacle of poetry finally achieved. "Don't give a dose to the one you love mos' " is excellent advice, and it does rhyme, but by no stretch of the imagination can it be called poetry.

We may tend to forget that until the first few decades of the twentieth century the idiom of poetry was never the idiom of common speech. It was cast in a formal language often as stately and measured as prayer or chant; it was "high-sounding" if you will, which gave it a dignity and even a quasi-religious gravity men found impressive —and never mind what it might or might not be saying. Ezra Pound brought all this to a crashing—and well-deserved—end by insisting that poetry be cast in the language and rhythms of ordinary speech. Yet as one has watched the extremes to which that pendulum has swung one begins to ask some serious questions. If poetry is to be cast in common speech, whose common speech? There is a difference after all between such common speech as "what da hell you tink you're doing bud" and the common speech of "over the heavens, the clouds go, nevertheless, in their direction." Should poetry reflect the interests and mental capacities of the least educated or the best educated men? Above all, one finally asks: has stripping poetry of intellectual content and a formal idiom really succeeded in returning poetry to the people? And the answer to that, I think, is no.

R. E. Sebenthall

15

## 3

As one plods through the work of many young poets one feels the devaluation of the mind has gone about as far as it can go. On the one hand we find a flabby conversational tone, as lacking in perceptual as in intellectual content. On the other hand we find the shock-tactics older poets had already exhausted—fractured syntax, typographical lunacies, non-words, non-phrases, non-sense, surrealistic image-mazes going nowhere but to the bottom of the page, hallucinatory notations, sophomoric obscenities—the whole paraphernalia of an art seeking to reflect what it sees as a chaotic and senseless world by itself becoming as chaotic and senseless as possible. Unless one wants to linger forever in these over-worked fields the only road left, it appears, is one leading back to a recognition of poetry as something more than a refuge for the intellectually impoverished, as something more than a playground for pranksters and exhibitionists, as something more than a womb-tank for the gropers and feelers who have yet to learn how to establish the most rudimentary contact with anything outside themselves. Poetry is either serious communication about serious matters between serious people, or it is nothing at all.

Perhaps the first corrective step must be to admit that poetry, in any real sense of the word, will continue to appeal as it always has to only a relatively small and special audience—readers and listeners who value it as the distillation of a gifted and unusual person's life-experience, who are prepared to give as much care and attention to what a poet has to say as the poet spent on saying it, and who possess a sufficiently large frame of reference to grasp subtle and complex material. This would mean that poetry must once again be given the strength and toughness of intellectual content as well as the dignity of a formal idiom. Let me hasten to add that this last stipulation is in no sense a plea for a return to the stately and artificial language of the past. It merely asserts that commonplace language does not serve every poetic purpose. If the poet has something profound and subtle to say—and the best poets do—he cannot express it in the jargon of the streets, he cannot make it accessible or attractive to the man of limited mental capacity. Concision, tension, irony, and metaphorical richness have marked the best poetry of this century. They are achieved only by a probing mind, an able and vigorous intellect. And they are sacrificed, I think, only at the risk of straying from the mainstream.

4

Many young poets today have opted for a drastically different (if by no means new) life style. This is all to the good. The question is can they effectively communicate the value of what they have done? Can they even understand what there is about it that might be of interest to anyone but themselves and therefore worth trying to communicate? We are not going to be held enthralled forever by their living arrangements, their trips (acid or ego), their clothes, their hair, their jargon, their political and social credos. All this we know. What we want to know is whether, as a result of their changed life style, they have anything new to say about life, about the eternal questions and mysteries that have occupied the mind of man.

Charles Reich to the contrary, men and women of every generation have rejected the Establishment to explore the rewards of Consciousness III; have returned to nature, have dabbled in eastern mysticism, have sat in the sun all day for the sheer sensual pleasure of it, have believed that war was evil, government corrupt, society shallow and materialistic. Thoreau probably said everything there was to say about dropping out, about living the simple life in the woods. So what else is new? we are finally forced to ask: what else has the counterculture to tell us?

Ours is not (never was, of course) a simple world, and simplistic approaches do not really simplify it; they merely falsify it. The young poet needs every ounce of brains and knowledge, as well as every ounce of perceptual ability he can summon to even begin to grapple with the problems and ramifications of existence. Until he has grappled with them he has little if anything to offer. Perhaps one does not have a choice as to whether one will be a Rod McKuehn or an A. R. Ammons. One's abilities both as person and poet decide it, at least to some extent. Yet the formative years of the young poet can be directed, and if he is encouraged early to reject the past for an exclusive diet of Here and Now, if he is encouraged to consider sense-data his only reliable material, he has been handed very meager equipment with which to confront not only a complex and challenging world but a complex and challenging art.

Certainly if we are to assume that the counterculture will survive at all it seems safe to assume that, as with any culture, there will be considerable shifting of emphases, considerable change and growth in direction and values. It may, therefore, in all honesty be too early to expect what is at this point a youthful culture to begin showing the marks of maturity. Yet we can, in fairness, wonder at this point if its poets are accumulating the kind of tools and materials that will enable them to ever achieve a maturity. Here the evidence, based on a continuing trend toward antiintellectualism, suggests a discouraging answer. Whether ignorance is chosen or imposed, the fruits are the same: intolerance, narrowness of vision, inability to communicate with any but one's own kind. If the counterculture's poets are satisfied—or condemned—to speak only of and to those who share their outlook and values they are engendering a cultism that has little chance of standing the test of time.

Men reach heights by climbing on the shoulders of the giants who preceded them and endeavoring to perfect the instruments the giants used. To slay the giants and discard the instruments because both were less than perfect is the way of children or barbarians. It is as true today as ever that the most difficult and challenging task for a poet is to think a thought about this life and get it expressed. One can only hope that the poets of an evolving counterculture will recognize this fact and restore the intellect—that cleaver which discerns and rifts its way into the secret of things—to its rightful place as one of the most valuable and potent instruments a poet can possess.

# THE ARTISAN AS HERO

## 1. THE ARROW-MAKER

R. E.
*Sebenthall*
19

Forget art, never mind
the brain or the brawn.
It doesn't go back
to the wisest or best,
understand—the one who scratched
pictures on the cave wall or made
wild guesses on the lay of the bones,
nor to the biggest
and strongest. It goes back
to the clever-fingered brute
who sharpened the first stone.

It starts there and it's that simple.
There had to be something
that mattered more than anything else,
and the one thing that mattered
that much to all of them
was one more day at any price.

Take it from there and you see
why they let him sit in the shade—
him of the funny knack—
fooling with sticks and stones.
Back of the stupid eyes,
deep in the earliest brow,
they knew what the thinkers
still can't think around.

# 2. THE POTTER

R. E.
Sebenthall

20

Jug, bowl, cup, bottle—
no cunning gets you past
the basic cave and entrance.
So let's say it was a she,
though we can't guess
how many thousands of years
she bent over the curved leaf
that held the water, the cupped
hand, her own round belly—
and nothing went pop
in the slow thick porridge
at the top of her skull.

We can't name the day when she
picked up the handful of mud
and happened to shape it
round and hollow. Later
saw it lying where she'd dropped
it—sun-baked and full of water.
So did it again and went
picking berries with it,
and never knew she had bumbled
onto civilization.

It's still in a mothering
of hands, a craft of caress
as the wheel turns
that the shape takes place.

## 3. THE WEAVER

It came late. It's sophisticated,
a luxury. Skins, crude knots and lashings
were adequate. They didn't
really need this. And somebody
had to think two things at once
before it could happen.
Somebody had to notice the mystery
of opposites: dark and light,
male and female, earth and sky.
Somebody had to feel the split
of good and evil in his gut.
Somebody had to sadden
on separation.

It moves away from mere
usefulness. It gets
abstract. Don't let fish nets,
traps and baskets confuse
what the troubled one was up to
when he sat plaiting
two thongs or reeds, making
nothing in particular that time,
but easing an ache
he barely knew he had.

Among pots and arrows,
somebody had begun
the long agony
of reconciliation.

R. E.
*Sebenthall*
21

# TWO NUNS ON A BEACH

R. E.
*Sebenthall*

22

God's big wind
pushing their prayers
back down their throats,
flapping their careful skirts,
does not bend
the tall white spars of their souls.

The edges of a whole ocean
of unspeakable mystery and violence
licking their decorous boots,
does not suggest
the possibility of more
than their gentle fences include.

They step around what doesn't fit,
climb over the contradictions, skip
the heathenish howl of the sun,
gulls screaming indecencies,
the sand littered with foul murder,
the brazen couple, naked and urgent,
back of the rock.

Out in that savage,
beaten and walloped,
their equanimity does not fail.

They stride along,
they seem to enjoy it;
they are buoyant
as small tight boats in a gale.

# UNDER THE VOLCANO

## 1

R. E.
Sebenthall
23

Brain-colored, but stupidly inquisitive as sheep,
clouds wander up, bunt the long dirty scarves of smoke

with whey-wet noses, rub clabber-soft bellies
on the lethal lips. So children play with a cocked gun,

but live, mostly. Utterly oblivious of how many
permissions are involved, by what a number

of gratuitous suspensions and abstentions
we do so, we, the glittering people, debouch

from the pulsing pueblos for a day by the sea.
Calmly assuming we would not be dismissed

without a preliminary bang, it is safe this morning
to suppose we will be accommodated with oxygen,

that the solar system will respect our plans, and
the volcano not go off to spoil things.

It is safe to suppose that for no particular reason
the world will turn just so fast and no faster.

It is safe to assume comets and stars are on track.
That time and tide will honor the ancient agreements.

R. E.
Sebenthall

24

By those ancient agreements we may walk here,
and the sea take no more than what is the sea's.

But the sand burns with a furtive resentment.
Splinters of light are hating our special eyes.

Sandwiched between the visceral furnace
and the sky's inferno, how thin the layer of lief

that befriends us. How little the crabs and gulls
appear to be impressed with our importance.

Perhaps it is time to examine our conscience.
We are old and rich. What is there to say in our favor?

Marauders and spoilers, posers, fakers,
dragging our bag of murder and self-forgiveness by proxy,

we have never been really liked. The sky
could start down like the half of a closing mussel.

Those tendrils of smoke turn quietly rosy with deaths.
And the sea that throws up such specialties,

such lumbering stalk-eyed things. . . . Do we really know if
its final ghastly surprise has shambled up from the beach?

3

Swept in on an accident, and for the moment overlooked,
our crowns rest easily nevertheless. We do not question

R. E.
*Sebenthall*
25

ourselves, nor notice we are crumbling slowly
in an air that only happened to be here.

We do not observe that we sit in a circle of glares.
We ignore the pistol pressed to the back of our head.

Here is our lunch and our paperback; these are our reasons.
We've brought our salvation; it is safe to relax.

Our flesh is guarded with grease, our watches
muzzle eternity, our dark glasses tame the truth.

Back of their shepherding panes we have fallen asleep.
Our minds lie limp as punctured beach balls.

Our souls are drying sponges. We're doped and dull.
We're plain and brute in brute enough. Unhelped,

the sky rolls on. Unasked, a world's provided.
We turn and toast. We loll and are. We stay all day.

The sea, tortured with could, but honor-bound,
continues to arrive and go away.

# THE EXISTENTIALIST

R. E.
*Sebenthall*
26

works twice as hard as anyone else:

every morning has to swim out
and bring back the boats
every night carries off: and since

his house isn't plugged in
to the conveniences,
meanings have to be lugged
from the spring, warmth
coaxed from two sticks,

and right in the middle of
roof-patching or chink-calking
he may have to go off
looking for his reasons

which won't be
the sort of thing
you pick up at the store

but some hard-to-find
even accidental trifle
like cricket-chirr
in November grass
or the color
of the cock pheasant's neck
as it breaks from the brush.

## THE PARANOIAC

Cast out long ago, he has forgotten
whether he is trying to be lost
or found. Caught in a limbo between them,
like a nervous lizard
between shade and shade,
his morsel dares inhabit
nobody long, and he darts
through such malignant countries

that he often cleverly hides himself
in the baggage he carries—
jars of excreta, packets
of nail clippings and shorn hair.
What enemy would imagine these
worth hauling before the tribunal?
Even death, no dolt,
searching the world for the man
would come away foiled.

At no time can he risk knowing his real name
which he keeps in a vial up his anus,
or face the deadly trap of a camera.
He is always awake, holding
the phone taps and computers at bay,
minding his occupational necessities—
to be small and still when the spies
of Palomar aim their giant gazes,
to be large and fast when the fanged
curs of love snap at his ankles.

After years of such grim cloak-and-dagger
he has polished his magic
beyond belief; can stop time
with a wave of his wand,
pull kings and armies from his hat,
run faster than light, or vanish
entirely into Napoleon or God.

R. E.
*Sebenthall*
27

# SAYING IT

R. E.
*Sebenthall*
28

Who knows what determines
the particular things
you'll decide to mention?
The sly wigwagging of this
or that indirect or oblique
happens so far down
it's beyond being sure.
Something just waves
greatly from the jammed
signalling of welter:
you answer: it's yours.

Out in stone-last, hill-stay,
fox-sneak, the arrangement
of two tamarack against a sky,
or ducks riding November lakes,
who knows what will flash up
from all that flux
with the sudden sting of statement?

Is it even you out looking
for a poem that finds it,
or is the lean soul of motion
after your verbs? Something
sends, something receives,
something uses or is used: that only
is clear. Beyond it, who knows
what speaks, what listens,
what arranges the words?

# CENSURE, WITH ONE MINOR RESERVATION

I don't forgive a single thing:
not one rat-bitten hungry child,
not one dead lake or one bombed village,
not one slave or one vanished species,
nor one black toad of a big lie
squatting on all of us.

However, since shrimp and cabbages
have degrees of failure, too.
since sparrows and lions
do not always achieve
their potential, I acknowledge

I should not have assumed
an ability to imagine perfection
was anything more
than a trail rambling
pointlessly away
over a scarred slope
in an unlikely direction.

*R. E.*
*Sebenthall*
29

HANGING LOOSE

R. E.
Sebenthall

30

Maybe the backyard crew
does it better—no nonsense
about mavericks and different
drummers, but all hands straight on
down the iron track: the robin
clamped in a groove
between worm and nest,
the ant never stopping
whatever ants do, the bee at its
dip, load up, back to the hive
in a line so strict it has a name.

So it gets things done. But
I'll take the way
the human can drop
out of the story—
waste time, walk on the beach,
stare and muse, accomplish nothing
in an air where the status
of drudges has fallen
and nobody remembers the busy beavers
who didn't go off to loaf at Walden.

BIBLIOGRAPHY

*Biographical Note.* Born in Eau Claire, Wis. Author, under several pseudonyms, of over a dozen novels, mostly in the mystery and suspense field. Following publication of poetry collection, recipient of a 1970 National Endowment for the Arts Discovery Award Grant.

R. E.
Sebenthall
31

POETRY COLLECTION

*Acquainted With A Chance of Bobcats,* Rutgers University Press, New Brunswick, N.J., 1969

MAGAZINE APPEARANCES

*Thoreau,* The Colorado Quarterly, 1961
*Consummation,* The Beloit Poetry Journal, 1961
*The Baddies,* The Beloit Poetry Journal, 1962
*Explorer,* The Beloit Poetry Journal, 1962; reprinted in New York Times Book Review, 1962
*Easter Island,* Kenyon Review, 1963
*Crows,* The Beloit Poetry Journal, 1963
*The Killer,* Epoch, 1964
*Lone Wolf,* The Massachusetts Review, 1965
*Pharoah,* The Western Humanities Review, 1965
*Book Burners,* The Western Humanities Review, 1966
*The Chinese,* The Western Humanities Review, 1966
*Wild Geese,* Perspective, 1966
*Hans Christian Andersen,* Perspective, 1966
*Acquainted With A Chance of Bobcats,* Perspective, 1966
*The Sieves,* Perspective, 1967
*Under The Volcano,* Perspective, 1967
*The Holy Indigents,* The Western Humanities Review, 1967
*Ivory Tower,* The Human Voice, 1968
*Cuckoo House,* Perspective, 1968
*Two Nuns On A Beach,* Perspective, 1968
*Fiftieth Anniversary,* Perspective, 1968
*Variations On A Theme By Rilke,* Poetry Northwest, 1969
*Three Notes On Brevity,* The Human Voice, 1970
*Mandarin,* The Human Voice, 1970
*Transplants,* St Andrews Review, 1971
*Last Words,* St. Andrews Review, 1971
*The Artisan As Hero,* The Western Humanities Review, 1971
*The Atavists,* St. Andrews Review, 1972
*The Prophets,* Perspective, 1972
*Main Street,* Perspective, 1972
*Nativities,* Perspective, 1972

## ANTHOLOGY APPEARANCES

R. E.
Sebenthall

32

Borestone Mountain Anthology, Best Poems of 1967
Borestone Mountain Anthology, Best Poems of 1971
New Poetry Out of Wisconsin, Sauk City, Wis.
Our Only Hope Is Humor, Some Public Poems, Ashland Poetry
  Press, Ashland, Ohio
The Human Voice Anthology, 1969

## REVIEWS and ARTICLES of:

Library Journal, Oct. 15, 1969
Capitol Times, Madison, Wis., 1970
The Human Voice, 1970
St. Andrews Review, Fall-Winter, 1970
Milwaukee Journal, Milwaukee, Wis., 1970
The Denver Quarterly, Summer 1970
The Booklist, July 15, 1970
Parade of Books, May 10, 1970
The Sunday Star, Washington, D.C., Aug. 16, 1970
New Dominion Magazine, The Daily Press, Newport News, Hampton, Vt., July 10, 1970

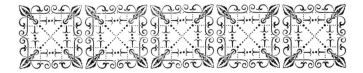

POETRY AND PLACE:

AN INTERVIEW WITH THOMAS McGRATH

The following interview was conduct-
ed by Mark Vinz at Moorhead State
College on July 25, 1972.

*Vinz*: I'd like to know how you feel about a "sense of
place" in poetry, particularly in your own poetry .

*McGrath*: I don't think that my sense of the importance
of "place" has to do with regionalism as such. I do think
that if I lived somewhere else I would have the same
sense of the importance of the place I was in, and I
would want to know something about it. I would want to
know it not just in a historical sense. I would want to try
to live in the landscape of the place.

The reason I don't think this is possible very much
in the East — at least in the city — is that you can't form
the same kind of an associations with a street or street
corner that you can with a piece of landscape, a river or
a lake, or something of this sort. You can form certain
relationships, it's absolutely true. That is, if you grow up
"on a corner," that is going to be very important to you,
but what you have there are *human* relationships, your
own personal history, and so on; you have no sense, I
think, of the history of that particular corner in relation
to the city. And of course you can't have any sense of a
relationship to nature at all. You can't have any sense of
a relationship to processes that are extra-human process-

es, processes which seem to me very important — that is, seasonal changes, the growth in the desert thing, and so on.

This seems to me enormously important — these very old earth rhythms — to a writer. I think that is a primary thing. I'm not interested in nature in a nineteenth century sense — I don't have any pantheistic feelings about nature, I don't have any nature mysticism, I believe. I don't see nature as representing some kind of higher order of things. It's just for me something that's there, that is the ground of man's existence, and I think that without some sense of the goings-on of nature — things like the seasonal changes, growth and death, and so on — a whole dimension of one's life is missing.

Everybody knows about the ltitle boy who goes out into the country and discovers for the first time that milk doesn't come out of a bottle or a carton. It's something to do with that. I don't know how to say this, but I believe there is something very deep in us that needs this kind of thing — we need to be able to find ourselves, at times, in this most ancient order of things, because it tends to give us some sense of perspective — so that's a part of it.

The other thing that is important to me: I do have a strong sense of wanting to know something about what has gone on in a place, and that is difficult in the East, because while there is a great deal of past history there, there are essentially no elements of it left; whereas out here, and farther west and southwest, you can get very strongly that sense. The southwest, I think, might be particularly marvellous. It's not essentially the kind of climate or country that I like, but there's something great in New Mexico and Arizona in what remains — first of all the actual daily lives of the Indians there. They're still an enduring part of the landscape. Also in the old ruins of places like Keet Seel, Batatikan, Mesa Verde, and so on. You are continually reminded there that you are just a moment in a history that goes very far back, and God knows how far it will go into the future, if there is a future.

This, I think, again has something to do with the sense of perspective or distancing in relation to your own particular projects, which are very short ones looked at on a bigger time-scale.

That's part of it. For me there's something very moving and meaningful about the fact that *here* you can go out to the North Dakota Sand Hills and you pick up an arrowhead and that arrowhead might have been shot at my grandfather. You know, that kind of thing — the sense of the past *being* here, not so much in social institutions, because most of that is gone, but in terms of something more enduring than that: the landscape itself.

So I'm not at all interested in the region merely as a region — that is, I don't think there's anything special about the Midwest, the Northwest, the Upper Midwest, the Southwest, or any single place. I don't think any *one* of these places is more meaningful than another, and I don't think that the values of these regions are particularly *regional* values. Do they exist at all? Regional values? I don't know that they do, really. They are only variants of national values and I reject national values, so I have to reject the *particular* way in which those are expressed, the parochial expressions of these things that one finds in a region. Does that answer you?

*Vinz*: Yes, I think so . . . .

*McGrath*: It's still very hard to say, to come to grips with this business of *place*. One thing, that of course is meaningful to any poet, I believe, is that a sense of place is a way of anchoring the poem somewhere. And I think many poems grow out of place even though they may be on subjects that seem to have nothing whatsoever to do with place. There is no overt element of place in them, but nevertheless, I think, they do grow out of place just the same. That doesn't answer it either, but it's in there somewhere.

*Vinz*: What about your particular relation with North Dakota? I've heard you tell the younger people around here the words "Dakota experience" — I can't remember whether it's in the long poem [*Letter to an Imaginary Friend*] or not, but Robert Bly mentioned William Stafford saying that "Kansas is everywhere," and you've been quoted as saying that "Dakota is everywhere."

*McGrath*: In the long poem, [Letter] I do say "Dakota is everywhere." I was writing that while we were on Skyros, and if you look at that first section of the poem you will find that there is a great deal of *place* in terms of Skyros in that section. The poem continually returns to North Dakota and looks at particular things — a certain sort of sacred ground for me, the old coulee, the river, and so on — these are the "gates" that Bob talked about. And while that "return" is a recurrent thing, I always have in the poem not just the narrative line but also the *immediate* thing, with references to what is immediately "outside the window," because the poem is also the *writing* of the poem.

Well, let's see what we were talking about — oh, Dakota is everywhere. The thing that set off that particular section in Skyros was this: I had gone there by chance. We might have gone somewhere else in Greece — but we were there, and I had some time.

I was going to work on the long poem, and so I started working on it, and one of the things that happened the first or the second night we were there was that a fisherman hanged himself. Somebody so poor — the fishermen in Skyros are the poorest in Greece, and fishermen in Greece are all of them poor.

Anyway, this was a thing that happened. It came into the poem; it became part of the poem and it is a kind of theme that is picked up and carried through to the end of part two. Obviously I couldn't very well have planned on the suicide; it was there, and I used it, and when I wrote the line "Dakota is everywhere" I was thinking as much of that suicide as of anything else. But I meant a particular kind of condition — that is the condition of oppression, and of class struggle. The conditions of poverty and war and anguish don't belong to any particular place, but they were part of my experience in North Dakota, and in that sense Dakota is everywhere.

In one way I believe that one could say, if one grew up in Kansas, "Kansas is everywhere." Because the experience that we have — if it's not a limited, parochial experience, if it's a wide enough experience — the experience that we have in *one* place will fit most of the world. At least if we have the experience of poverty and deprivation and so on, *that* will fit most of the world. If we have the experience of growing up rich somewhere, that *won't* — it would be a more limited kind of experience. But what I emphasized by the expression "Dakota is everywhere" was not just *place* but *experience.*

Now this business, the "Dakota experience," whatever it is — there are certain things in it. I don't claim it merely for North Dakota, or even for that "Dacotah Territory" that you've mapped out, which is much bigger than Dakota. I would say that it is the experience that would be true for all states that are dominated by the land itself and not by the city or by the machine or the factory. And so it would be a kind of experience that one might have had in Oklahoma or Texas, or in Kansas, Nebraska or in South or North Dakota or Montana and the mountain states. It would be true of that whole great stretch west of the Mississippi.

The only thing that I would except from it would be the extreme west coast. I would except from it California in some parts — the cities anyway: that city strip that will someday run completely along the coast from San

Diego up to Seattle. That's a different kind of experience. There's a difference in what happened out there too. Eastern culture went around the Horn and wound up in San Francisco. San Francisco, with all its differences, was in many ways an eastern city rather than a western one. It had opera, for example. It has and always had a tradition of the arts and culture — as compared to Los Angeles, say, which didn't.

What happened in between the coasts was a different kind of experience. A culture that evolved out of immigrants, that's the first thing. It was a culture which was not conditioned or modified by the arts. It was a non-book culture. The only book really of significance was the Bible. I have a vision of how this whole thing happened. You know: the covered wagon train is coming across and it is attacked by Indians, and the horses start galloping and they are running and running and the Indians are still gaining, so they start throwing out everything. They threw out the grandfather clock, so that time disappears; they threw out the old ormolu dingus, so the kitchen arts and the house arts disappear. And eventually they throw out Grandma, because it would lighten the load, and they throw out that copy of Shakespeare that nobody has read, and what are they left with? They're left with a rifle, the wife, and the Bible, and when they shake off the Indians that's what they've got and that's what they start with — that and the plow, of course.

Also the West, the extreme West, is older of course, much older, than the middle states. There are other things here: a populist politics, which was very strong out here and which led some people farther along the road into syndicalism, socialism, wobblyism. Later to communism and so on.

There is that very *American* kind of radicalism that grew up out here and that I think colored all the other movements. It colored syndicalism, for instance, and the wobblies here had a strong western and agrarian bias. It

colored socialist thinking; it colored communist thinking — even though essentially the communists were Marx-
ist, their particular attitudes were very much of the west,
of the open country. So the Dakota experience comes out
of things like that.

There are many, many other things that I haven't got
to — the Puritanism, for instance, of most of these states.
That's a piece of it too. It's something that not just every
writer but every*body* has had to fight against to some degree or other. All the kids had to fight against it, you
know, and a good many of them, of course, abandoned
the fight very early and sat down to a kind of existence
where they accepted, verbally anyway, the prohibitions
and restrictions of these puritanical churches. But nevertheless, that's there — both the fact of the puritanism and
the fact of the struggle against it is there.

Other things, too. The primary experience out in these
states, originally anyway, was an experience of loneliness,
because the people were so far away from everything.
They had come out here and left behind whatever was
familiar, and you find this again and again in letters that
women wrote out here. The other side of that loneliness
was a sense of community, which was much more developed — even as late as thirty or forty years years ago
— than it is now. The community of swapped labor. This
was a standard thing on the frontier; everybody got together and helped put up a house or put up a soddy when
a new family came along. You helped with this, that or the
other, and you swapped labor back and forth all the time
in that particular little community in which you lived;
and that community was never defined. It wasn't a geo-
graphical thing; it was a sort of commune of people who
got along well together, and right in the same actual
neighborhood there might be two or three of these.

But that was one of the valuable things, that sense
of solidarity with the neighbors — even such things as social life were much more developed then than they are

now. It was much more developed when I was a boy than it is now. But even now, I think, there is still more than one finds in the cities. That's as far as I can go at the moment.

*Vinz*: One other question in this vein, and that is something we've been talking about, this whole idea of the experience of the past. You mentioned a "locus of the imagination." Do you think that that is true of Dakota for you, in light of what you said?

*McGrath*: It is for me.

*Vinz*: It's something you keep coming back to in *Letter to an Imaginary Friend*. This is what you mentioned before, this idea of a certain kind of perspective.

*McGrath*: Yes, that is absolutely true for me. It took me a while to find that out, because I wasn't able for a long time to make use of this — from the beginning I had written some poems which had to do with place, and I had to use images of place to at least some degree, but it wasn't until I started the long poem that I began to be able to use a lot of my personal experience; and I don't mean using it simply in the sense of writing it down, but using it in order to *see* things that I hadn't been able to see, really, before.

The most obvious thing was to be able to use things from my childhood and actually write them into the long poem. But I don't think that that was primary. It was that I had located in myself this something-or-other that was related to this particular area, and once I had put together that experience and the place, then there were many, many things that I was able to see that I hadn't been able to see before.

*Vinz*: One other thing in relation to this is what you said before about the past — this idea of searching back to something to get beyond the falsehood.

*McGrath*: It isn't at all because I idealize the past. If the past had been ideal we wouldn't have such a lousy present. I don't think that I sentimentalize that past at all. I don't *feel* sentimental about it, but I do feel that there *were* certain values that have been lost — at least temporarily lost — that existed.

This sense of solidarity there that I was talking about in the community is one of the richest experiences that people can have. It's the only true shield against alienation and deracination and it was much more developed in the past than it is now. Maybe in the future it will redevelop. One of the things that we are seeing now in the development of communes and so on, is exactly that: this uncounscious sense of a need for human solidarity, of the need for breaking out of the atomic isolationism of the lone individual or the lone family. Well, that was there.

Also, another thing that existed in the past was, I think, a different attitude toward work. It seems to me that while the work of the people who homesteaded here was backbreaking work, somehow or other people's attitude toward that work was a happier one than the attitude toward work now. I think the reason was that, for a while anyway — up until perhaps the end of the second world war — the sense that the farm and the whole farm community and the whole world of farming was . . . well, there was a kind of a dignity about it even during the time of the depths of the depression. There *was* a sense of this.

What happened after the second world war was that people here seemed to realize all at once, or to sense all at once, that they were just out on the *edge* of things and the real *image* became a city image and the middle class image.

There are a number of reasons for this. One, a new generation of farmers had come along. Two, the war had brought a kind of prosperity that they hadn't seen here for years. But probably the most important thing of all was this: television came along, and you could see into that world that before was so far away that you couldn't even imagine it. You could actually *see*, on television, New York or London, or this or the other. And of course what you were seeing on television (in all the television dramatic things) you were seeing the inside of the upper middle class houses, and you were seeing middle class people. Have you ever seen a farmer on television, outside of locally?

*Vinz*: Not the real ones.

*McGrath*: No, and something — that new image — began to dominate the image that people had of themselves. They began even to try to move toward it. I know of this very well from going to the houses of some of my friends — people with whom I had gone to high school — and suddenly I could see that I was walking straight into a *House and Garden* living room. Or: the really well off farmers began to go to Acapulco in the winters.

When I was a boy there was still an authentic peasantry, an Old Country peasantry. My grandfather was a peasant, and in many ways I suppose I am a peasant. But *that* has disappeared now — that world of the grandfathers, or even the fathers. My father was in many ways, I think, a peasant, even with his anarcho-syndicalism, because it was his own anarcho-syndicalism. It wasn't developed, it wasn't theoretical — it just occured by chance because he ran into the Wobblies.

And of course, historically, it's the peasants and the extreme bottom fringe of the lower middle class who have been attracted to anarchism. The anarchial syndicalist unions frequently were organized out of peasants who had just been recently proletarianized, and who had recently come into the factories. Anyway, there's a kind of indi-

vidualism about it that fits the peasant individualism. I
guess we've gotten off the subject somewhat.

*Vinz*: No, I don't think so — it's all related to the sense
of place in your work. I know that when you wrote some
things for me for *Dacotah Territory* you talked about this
being a good place to be, part of which you've already covered. Do you think there is any kind of "movement"
among younger writers to get out of the cities and find
particular *places* (not necessarily the Midwest)?

*McGrath*: I think absolutely that there is. I think it is very
strong and that it is closely related to the commune thing.
It's maybe a little more conscious, because the poet may
have a little more sense of why he wants to do this, but
I think it is a very, very strong thing. And one of the
things I think we were saying the other day when we were
talking with Bob Bly, is the fact that the young guy now
doesn't feel the same kind of isolation that I felt when I
was a kid interested in writing. You couldn't even find
the books that you wanted then. If you had wanted to be
a painter where the hell would you have gone to look at
painting in North Dakota, Minnesota, South Dakota, or
Montana? *That* was the attraction of the city. Culture was
there — I don't mean it in a limited sense, I mean it in
a factual sense. Libraries were there, bookstores were
there, museums were there. And so, the great need to go
because all of us felt terribly the limitations of small town
communities, the limitations of our *own* communities.
    We felt this in many ways. I have mentioned the puri-
tan business — that, I think, almost any artist probably
felt strongly. And the sense of not being able to talk to
anybody about those things that interested you most. It
was years and years before I came across a poet, before
I really talked to a poet. I think that the first poet that
I ever talked to was Bly — that's how long it was. No,
I'm wrong about that, but it wasn't for a long, long time.

Of course, I knew Alan Swallow, that's true. But in a sense he was in the same boat that I was in. I thought of a "poet" as somebody who had written a lot of poems and was going to go on writing poems, and who had written successful poems and probably published a book or two — this kind of thing is what I meant. And I didn't find them until I met people like Ed Rolfe and Don Gordon after I went out to the Coast. I had met a few others in England, it's true, but it wasn't really until about 1950 that I could say that I had spent time "talking with the poets."

Anyway, that's one of the things that sent people off to the cities. And now, for the kids the city is not some distant enchanted sort of place. First of all, they've seen them on television, they have that kind of familiarity with them. Secondly, they have enough money now — or most college kids do — so that if they want to go, if they want to make the run to — well, a few years ago to Haight-Ashbury, or San Francisco, New York, Seattle, or wherever—they can just do it. They can just hitchhike out and stay for two weeks or a month, or whatever — something we couldn't do. We could hitchhike, it's true; I remember one trip that we made — terrible, cold trip — to Chicago, which I guess was the first time I had seen an art gallery. I was well along in college at the time, and it was the first time I saw an honest-to-God bookstore, but of course I was too broke to buy any books. That was our problem. We could hitchhike, all right, and we knew how to live on nothing, but you *had* nothing — so that to go, to spend a summer or a month, or whatever, in a city was an impossible thing, or next to impossible for us, unless we had relatives there. You couldn't bank on getting a job because there was so much unemployment, and so on.

Well, now the kids make that run — they go there, they see San Francisco or wherever it is —and they discover that it isn't anything so special after all. There are bookstores everywhere now, with the kind of books they want if they are writers. There are enough established poets around in the empty spaces out here so that if the urge to talk with one of them overcomes them, they get into the car and they go down and bug Bly or whoever it happens to be — whatever poet they happen to be digging.

So the city doesn't have that same attraction. They go there and many of them return, because now the city has become such a goddamned ugly place, so hard to live in; that's one of the things that puts them off. And also there's something in the wind now that makes them more interested in the country than in the city. I don't know what the answer to that is; part of it is probably this business of wanting natural things, and it has resulted in the development of communes and all kinds of odd things like the macrobiotic diet, health food stores, organic gardening, and so on. But the number of kids, for instance, who are dreaming of having enough land so that they can do subsistence farming — that sends cold chills up my spine, since that's the only kind of farming that I have experienced, really, and not out of choice. It's an extremely hard thing for them to do, but they are very stubborn and they keep dreaming about doing this.

That, to me, is a very interesting thing, and the result is going to be — call it a renaissance or whatever term you like. It's already here. How big it will be, how long it will go, I don't know. But it's certainly something that's taking place now. Almost anywhere you look, you find these kids. Generally they have some kind of relationship to a local college or university, or to a local bohemia. But they're here, and in very substantial numbers, and with a surprising degree of proficiency, too.

*Vinz*: I have one more question, and that is, I guess, part of everything we have been talking about here and before. To be specific, it was in terms of something that you said in the fall when we were talking about the long poem: the idea of masks and the use of the first person. Somebody had commented that the use of the first person seemed very romantic, and you made a statement about this, which was also related in a way to *place*.

*McGrath*: Nobody would fuss about the use of first person in a novel. It is just a convention, and everybody accepts that without calling it romantic, or whatever. I think the convention may be applied more or less to the poem. There are times when the "I" really refers to me and to a particular piece of experience, and very often this is tied to a notation — I am here at this desk and outside the window is a tree, and that kind of thing.

Then, there are areas in the poem where I am telling something that has happened to an "I." Certainly, to a degree that *is* myself, but it would be a mistake to think that every time that "I" is used in the book it refers to a particular McGrath that is easily identifiable. Put it this way: I'm not interested in my personal experience simply as *personal* experience. I am interested in it even more insofar as it is also *representative* experience. So the "I" is in part a kind of mask; but it is easier to talk out of it than to talk out of something else.

What else could I do? I don't know how else you can write and still have the basis of the poem be narrative and to a degree autobiographical or pseudo-autobiographical. But I want to say this quite strongly, that this is no simple *autobiography*. There are things that have happened to me and that I have made use of, but there are many, many other things that have happened to me that I have made no use of whatsoever, and there are sections of the poem which are elaborated in the way that they could be if I were writing a novel and making use of a grain of experience that I had somewhere. The time, for instance, in the poem — that is, just the gross narrative time — is not accurate in the sense that you could say this year he was here and this happened, and that year he was there and that happened; it's not accurate in that sense. So that I would say that the "I" in the poem, while it sometimes is myself, is often a kind of mask which I use in order to try to get out of the piece of experience that I am dealing with the maximum effect, the greatest consciousness-expanding element that I can get.

Also, masks have other uses. The old Greek mask was a kind of a megaphone. One of the modes of this poem is exaggeration, and I don't know whether that's a piece of my personality — to exaggerate and elaborate some things — but I know that in parts of the poem it is something that comes along and that I think is truly a mask; I don't think that exaggeration is essentially a part of my thing, but exaggeration in terms of language, the exaggeration of certain kinds of actions to the point where they become surreal, fantastic—yes. I am thinking particularly of the section that has to do with the description of the tail end of winter and the beginning of spring during the thirties, during the dust storms, where various things were said about winter and what spring was like, and so on. That is exaggerated in the way of the tall tale.

But I think of that if I think of it at all — as a kind of a literary device that's been used by all kinds of people. It seems to me that I have several voices that come to me at times when I — or I hope when I — need them. And these are, some of them, voices out of the ground, voices of the place.

*Vinz*: What about this idea that you mentioned before, and you mentioned it just now — the representative experience, or that there are certain "configurations" that we all share?

*McGrath*: Yes, I think that everybody leads at least two lives: one as a unique individual with experience that no one else has and nobody else can have; and yet at the same time that he is having that unique experience, he is having, also, many times, the same kind of experience that someone else is having. That is to say, we are all born and the experience is unique to us, but it is an experience that everybody has.

What I am interested in is some kind of a story about a man who has lived through a certain stretch of time and who has experienced particular things. Now insofar as these things are unique things only, I am not essentially interested in them, but I *am* interested in the uniqueness of a representative act or the uniqueness of a represnta-tive experience. If I have the experience, let us say, of my first sexual encounter — now that is unique, yet it is also something that "everybody" has at some time. Insofar as it is unique and simply mine, I won't be talking to many people, but insofar as that experience is of the order of things where people can say "yes, that happened to me — not precisely this way, but I can enter that experience, I recognize that, that's the way it was" — that is the kind of thing that I am interested in.

And of course from a political standpoint, in terms of the politics of the poem, I am much interested in this, too, because I think very strongly — I *hope* very strongly — that the poem *is* a consciousness-expanding device. I think that the most terrible thing is the degree to which we carry around a *false* consciousness, and I think of poetry as being primarily an apparatus, a machine, a plant, a flower, for the creation of a *real* consciousness — at least a more real consciousness than the ones most people *have,* because most people can't orient themselves in re-lation to their lives. They don't know what the hell is go-ing on, because they can't locate themselves, they have never seen a map of where the hell they are but they are in Hell. They don't know which way is north, and this is specially true in political terms in this country. And since I've lived a long life — it began earlier than most people's lives — and had certain representative political experi-ences in my past, it seems to me that they are useful; any-way, I hope so.

# REMEMBERING LOVES AND DEATHS

They happened in us . . .
But later we moved away —
Or they did.

*Thomas
McGrath*
49

Went west.
Went south to the goldfields.
Disappeared somewhere beyond Salt Lake or Denver —
Their roads are still in the map of our flesh:
Easy to get to almost any time
Around midnight.

But the land shifts and changes, the map
Gets out of date,
The century stretches its joints,
And one day we stand by the marked tree and ask:
    *was it here*
*Was it here*
While, stunned but tireless,
Memory, the lodestone that always points toward pain,
Hunts, slow and sluggish for its North,
Turning through the thickening crystals of tired flesh
That was pure honey, once.

# THE HISTORIES OF MORNING

*Thomas*
*McGrath*
50

Morning spells light in the language of alarm clocks.
The streets bulge with ambition and duty,
Inhaling the populace out of exhausted houses.
The drowsy lion of money devours their calendars
In an absent-minded orgy of universal togetherness.

Meanwhile back among the ranch-type ramblers
The television set loosens the apron strings
Of housewives temporarily widowed
By that same quotidian lion of hard labor.

Now they are carried away by bowlegged heroes
To covered wagon livingrooms of the openfire range
Where the Masked Man turns out to be an old lover.

Somewhere — in the kitchen — the coffee is chuckling
    like Pandar.
Somewhere the factories shake in the fists of the workers.

# THE RETURN

The trees are never the same
             twice                          *Thomas*
                    the animals            *McGrath*
                          the birds or      51
The little river lying on its back in the sun or the sun or
The varying moon changing over the changing hills
Constant.
             It is this still that most I love about them.

I enter by dark or day:
                    that green noise, dying
Alive and living its death, that inhuman circular singing,
May call me stranger . . .
                    Or the little doors of the bark open
And I enter that other home outside the tent of my skin . . .

On such days, on such midnights, I have gone, I will go,
Past the human, past the animal, past the bird,
To the old mothers who stand with their feet in the loamy dark
And their green and gold praises playing into the sun . . .

For a little while, only. (It is a long way back).
But at least, and if but for a moment I have almost entered the stone.
Then fear and love call. I am cast out. Alien,
On the bridge of fur and of feather I go back to the world I have known.

# A NOTE ON THE LATE ELECTIONS

Behold, Friends, once more the Revolution has performed its famous
Disappearing act! And never before has one been preceded
By so many prophets! By so many holy books — all in translation!
By so many young men with long hair, so many poets with short
Breath!
     *And* the elephant bells!
        Oo la! And Incense
                                            *And*
The flowers!
     The flowers, alas, which never found the barrel
Of the gun that power grows out of.


                        And now the President, reborn
Out of the mystical body of the One and Universal
Voting machine, takes off the mask.
                     A thick and heavy
Darkness, like rust, is collecting in the amplified guitars.
The President will make the Airplane fly! He will make the
                                   Grateful Dead
Truly grateful! The President is casting the *other* I Ching.

A hard rain is falling; the roads are icing up.
And in every drop of the rain the sailors of the Potemkin sleep . . .

# DON'T THINK YOU KNOW MY NAME!

And so I am getting old!
Like a tree in the forest
I am shedding branches and leaves, and around my feet
Are enough dry twigs for three English martyrs —
And every son-of-a-bitch wants to set me on fire.

Not important of course. I'll have to walk out in the snow
In any case. Where else is there to turn?
So if you see me coming, a man made out of ice,
Splintering light like rainbows at every crazed joint of my
    body,
Better get out of the way: this black blood won't burn
And the fierce acids of winter are smoking in this cold
    heart.

*Thomas*
*McGrath*
*53*

Thomas
McGrath
54

## WHAT WAKES US

It was no dream —
Those great black doors
Rushing toward us
Through the dark.

## SURPRISE

He thinks it was all a mistake.
How could his faithful feet have carried him
(Never once leaving the marked and familiar trails)
To this strange place where everyone is dying?

## THINGS THAT ARE ENOUGH IN THEMSELVES

for Genya

That blizzard anchored in my yard —
The apple tree in blossom.
Damn all transcendence!
Say the honey bees and I.

---

I'll never get to where I'm going!
No surprise in that . . .
Plugging through this deep snow,
My arms continually around the dead . . .

---

To sit just downslope from the brow of a low hill
In the early evening.
To wait for the second song of the cricket —
What a great teacher you were
O my beloved father!

## ROUND SONG

My dead father comes back
In the shape of my little son.

And I sing him to sleep with his songs
Still in my own child's ear.

———————

My little son comes running with open arms!
Sometimes I can't bear it,
Father.
Did I, too,
Open your heart almost to breaking?

*Thomas*
*McGrath*
55

---

It is only when the leaves fall that we see
Where, all summer, clothed in the swarming light,
The hanged men swung in the wind.

---

# IN THE HILLS OF OLD WYOMING

For Marian
Powell, Wyoming, 1940

*Thomas McGrath*

The Bighorns are a perpetual metaphor:          57
Beside them anyone's speech is formal —
Exact as the little fields ruled off like
Crossword puzzles half worked out.

Below them water is tamed early and,
Charmed in circles, led around by the rows
Where work Mexicans with white teeth and huge
Delicate farmers whose dreams are literal.

Meanwhile over them and westward long
Breakers of light crash soundless on the Rockies:
Light spumed and splintered where the peaks' cold muzzles
Explore the avenues of frozen stars —

And I kept thinking that, if faith moved one,
My love would set the whole damned range to dancing.

# THE BUFFALO COAT

Thomas
McGrath
58

I see him moving, in his legendary fleece,
Between the superhighway and an Algonquin stone axe;
Between the wild tribes, in their lost heat,
And the dark blizzard of my Grandfather's coat;
Cold with the outdoor cold caught in the curls,
Smelling of the world before the poll tax.

And between the new macadam and the Scalp Act
They got him by the short hair; had him clipped
Who once was wild—and all five senses wild—
Printing the wild with his hoof's inflated script
Before the times was money in the bank,
Before it was a crime to be so mild.

But history is a fact, and moves on feet
Sharper than his, toward wallows deeper than.
And the myth that covered all his moving parts,
Grandfather's time had turned into a coat;
And what kept warm then, in the true world's cold
Is old and cold in a world his death began.

# THE NEWS AROUND MIDNIGHT

*Thomas
McGrath*
59

Past midnight now, and the city in its first heavy slumber
Lies on its right side.
              The stars ride forth.
                            The last
Quarter of the south-hung moon bars the skies with its
    light.
Cold light there for a fact and the late and empty streets
Cold in their dark and lack.
                      Now, on this hill, my window
Is a star, no farther. And still, in this Here, I spin my luck,
I work my light . . .

            *here,* at this table with the formica top,
As the despairing generations dream toward the day
Which can only be tomorrow, I prepare my spells
        and tools.

There is a planter here with a bit of green in it —
A cutting of Impatience which has just begun to root,
Some Mother-in-Law's Tongue, and a green shoot of
Leucojum just showing through — though I was a
    wild-rose man,
A Tiger Lily and Sassafras and Gooseberry man,
A man for the hill-hurdling crow calls and the cries of
    the kildeer
Falling through the green burden of the Autumn sundown
    woods.
But these are my tools now. These and my lonesome
    ghosts,
And the endless echoes of want in the lost streets of
    the terrible city.

Many nights you may see me here, around about midnight,
If you should look.
              Below me the city turns on its left
Side and the neon blinks in a code I can all too clearly

Read. It will go down with all hands.

Meanwhile

The moon steers and the stars wheel steady in the
ultimate North.

Thomas
McGrath

60 The ghosts sing round my light. Far in Dakota now
My father is dying. And here, in the silent house, in
shadowy
Rooms lying, my wife and children in their perfect sleep
Explore a darkness I can never reach.

I am

Necessary recorder.

A voice.

This sad machine —

It does little good, I know; still, I am here —

This sad machine: for love.

POEM

I don't belong in this century — who does?
In my time, summer came someplace in June —
The cutbanks blazing with roses, the birds brazen, and
    the astonished
Pastures frisking with young calves . . .
                    That was in the country —
I don't mean *another* country, I mean in the *country*:
And the country is lost. I don't mean just lost to *me,*
Nor in the way of metaphorical loss — it's lost that way
    too —
No; nor in no sort of special case: I mean
*Lost*

Now, down below, in the fire and stench, the city
Is building its shell: elaborate levels of emptiness
Like some sea-animal building toward its extinction.
And the citizens, unserious and full of virtue,
Are hunting for bread, or money, or a prayer,
And I behold them, and this season of man, without love.

If it were not a joke, it would be proper to laugh.
— Curious how that rat's nest holds together —
Distracting . . .
                    Without it there might be, still,
The gold wheel and the silver, the sun and the moon,
The season's ancient assurance under the unstable stars
Our fiery companions . . .
                    And trees, perhaps, and the sound
of the wild and living water hurrying out of the hills.

Without these, I have you for my talisman:
Sun, moon, the four seasons,
The true voice of the mountains. Now be
(The city revolving in its empty shell,
The night moving in from the East)
— Be thou these things.

*Thomas
McGrath*
61

# USED UP

*Thomas
McGrath*

62

1.

I remember the new-dropped colts in the time when I was
    a boy:
The steam of their bodies in the cold morning like a
    visible soul,
And the crimped hairy ring of warmed grass, first
    circle of sleep.
Spider-legged, later, they ate sugar from my shaken,
    scary hand.

2.

In a few more years they were broken: their necks
    were circled
With a farmer's need: with the dead leather legends and
    collars of their kin.
Gelded, the wild years cut out of them, harnessed
    to the world,
They walk the bright days' black furrows and gilded
    seasons of use.

3.

Now, dead; swung from the haymow track with block
    and tackle:
Gut-slit, blood in a tub for pigs, their skin dragged over
Their heads by a team of mules. Circlet of crows:
                            coyote song:
                            and bones
Rusting coulee moonlight: lush greenest spring grass
    where the body
Leaped.
            Three acts and death.
                    The horse
                                    rides
Into the earth.

SELECTED BIBLIOGRAPHY

Books

*First Manifesto,* Alan Swallow: Baton Rouge, 1940. (Swallow Pamphlet No. 1)

*Three Young Poets,* selected by Alan Swallow, The Press of J. A. Decker: Prairie City, Illinois, 1942.

*To Walk a Crooked Mile,* Alan Swallow: New York, 1947.

*Longshot O'Leary's Garland of Practical Poesie,* International Publishers: New York, 1949.

*Witness to the Times!,* privately printed, 1954.

*Figures from a Double World,* Alan Swallow: Denver, 1955, (Swallow poetry book award of 1954)

*The Gates of Ivory, The Gates of Horn,* with a foreword by Charles Humboldt, Mainstream Publishers: New York, 1957. (Novel)

*About Clouds,* illustrated by Chris Jenkyns, Melmont Publishers: Los Angeles, 1959. (Children's book)

*The Beautiful Things,* illustrated by Chris Jenkyns, Vanguard Press: New York, 1960. (Children's book)

*Letter to an Imaginary Friend,* Alan Swallow: Denver, 1962.

*New and Selected Poems,* Alan Swallow: Denver, 1962.

*Letter to an Imaginary Friend,* Parts I and II, Swallow Press: Chicago, 1970.

*The Movie at the End of the World — Collected Poems,* Swallow Press: Chicago, 1973.

*A Sound of One Hand,* Minnesota Writers Publishing House (in preparation for May, 1973)

Anthologies

*American Writing,* Press of James A. Decker, Prairie City, Illinois, 192. Edited by Alan Swallow.

*Cross Sections,* Simon and Schuster, New York, 1947. Edited by Edwin Seaver.

*New Poets of England and America,* World Publishing Co. Cleveland, Ohio, 1957. Edited by Donald Hall, Robert Pack, and Louis Simpson.

*Poetry of Los Angeles,* Villiers Publications, London, 1958. Edited by James Boyer May, Thomas McGrath, and Peter Yates.

*Pata Ronci Doba: Amerika Radikalni Roezie:* Mlada Fronta, Prague, 1959. Edited by Jan Zabrana.

*New Orlando Poetry Anthology:* Vol. 2. Greenwich Village, N.Y., 1963. Edited by Anca Vrbovska.

*Poets of Today: A New American Anthology,* International Publishing Co., New York, NY, 1964. Edited by Walter Lowenfels.

*San Francisco Renaissance: Ellere Moderne Amerikanske Lyrikere,* Sirius, Denmark, 1964. Edited by Erik Thygeson.

*Poems On Poetry — The Mirror's Garland,* E. P. Dutton & Co., 1965. Edited by Robert Wallace and James G. Taffe.

*Heartland, Poets of the Midwest,* Northern Illinois University Press, DeKalb, Illinois, 1967. Edited by Lucien Stryk.

*Where is Vietnam?*, Doubleday and Co., Garden City, NY, 1967. Edited by Walter Lowenfels.

*New Orlando Poetry Anthology*, Greenwich Village, NY, 1968. Edited by Anca Vrbovska, Alfred Dorn, and Robert Lundgren.

*Where Steel Winds Blow*, David McKay Co. Inc., New York, 1968. Edited by Robert Cromie.

*Contemporary Poets of the English Language*, St. James Press, Chicago and London, England, 1970.

*Forty Poems Touching on Recent American History*, Beacon Press, Boston, 1970. Edited by Robert Bly.

*Poetry for Pleasure, The Hallmark Book of Poetry*, Doubleday and Co., Garden City, NY, 1970.

*Poetry North Five Poets of North Dakota*, North Dakota Institute for Regional Studies, Fargo, ND, 1970. Edited by Richard Lyons.

*The Rebel Culture*, Dell Publishing Co., Inc., New York, 1970. Edited by Robert S. Gold.

*That Voice That is Great Within Us*, Bantam Books Inc., 1970. Edited by Hayden Carruth.

*Live Poetry*, Holt, Rinehart, and Winston Inc., New York, 1971. Edited by Kathleen Sunshine Koppell.

*Six Poets of the Red River*, Printed for "Imagination '71", Fargo, ND, 1971. Edited by Anthony Oldknow and Mark Vinz.

*Getting Into Poetry*, Rostan Holbrook Press Inc., 1972. Edited by Morris Sweetkind.

*Poets of the Red River*, Scopecraeft Press, Fargo, ND, 1972. Edited by Anthony Oldknow.

Tapes

LWO 2896, reel 6. Poems read for Radio Station KUSC, Los Angeles, 1958-1959 series.

LWO 317. Poems read at Radio Station KPFK, Los Angeles, Feb. 18, 1960.

Library of Congress recordings #455 and #456 as listed in *Literary Recordings, a Checklist of the Archive of Recorded Poetry and Literature in the Library of Congress*.

Tapes at Radio Station WBAI, New York (do not know index numbers) and in English Departments at NDSU (Fargo, ND) and Moorhead State College, (Moorhead, Minn.). Video tape or reading at St. Cloud State College, St. Cloud, Minn.

About the poet:

Born in North Dakota. Educated at University of North Dakota, Louisiana State University, and New College, Oxford University, where he was a Rhodes Scholar. Served in Air Force in the Aleutians during WWII. Has taught from time to time at colleges and universities in Maine, California, New York, North Dakota, and Minnesota. Between periods of teaching, was a free lance writer of fiction and film (mostly documentary). Held Amy Lowell Travelling Poetry Scholarship, 1966-67. Guggenheim Fellowship, 1967-68. Founder and first editor (with Eugenia McGrath) of the poetry magazine *Crazy Horse*. Married to Eugenia McGrath and has a son, Tomasito, age 4.

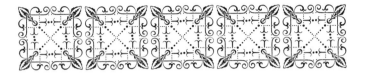

TO CREATE A FACE

*A Brief Essay on the Development of a Style*

AS I set down these notes, I am constantly plagued by a
line Robert Frost cadged from E. F. Forster, who got it
from an old lady: How do I know what I think until I
see what I say?"

This line is as fine a description of my problem when
functioning as literary theorist as it is a description of part
of my poetic process. Because I am not a professional
literary critic, though I have been an editor. And for all
that I have taught literature for 19 years, I am not a literary historian or sociologist or philosopher. I have only
that much skill with these arch disciplines as is sufficient
to my work as a poet and a teacher.

What I am is a writer—subspecies: poet.

All this by way of saying that I am not going to say
much about "Trends in American Poetry," because I don't
know much about such trends. That is a consideration for
the political pollster of literature or the literary historian.
If there are such things as *trends* in literature, and there
seem to be, a writer, since his art is solitary—a private
matter more like dying or making love than making out
one's income tax return, is likely to know little about them.
Either because he is part of a trend and, therefore, like
the passenger on a plane, unable to observe himself aloft.
Or because, his mind centered on his personal vision, he
is careless of such larger details.

I have been offered a nice latitude in this piece, and
propose to avail myself of it. I am free to talk about what

and how I feel about my own work (something I seldom indulge in), and how I see it relating or not to the Midwest, to contemporary ideas and stylistic influences. These are subjects I may legitimately pretend to some knowledge of.

As to *how* I feel about my work?

It depends on when you ask me the question.

If you ask just after I've finished a poem, and especially if the poem has turned out well, the answer is always, "Great!" How else would one feel? I suppose it's the same order and kind of feeling Willie Sutton might have had if he'd ever quarterbacked the Green Bay Packers. If you ask me the question when I'm in a slump, the answer is, "Rotten!" If you're a bootlegger, how do you feel when the still breaks down?

As to *what* I feel—that's a more complex question. So complex I'm not sure I can answer it, because what I feel about my own work varies from year to year, and because I'm fairly certain what I feel about my work is, in the last analysis, irrelevant to any discussion of the poems themselves.

I see myself as a poet;—I don't believe in poets as prophets, or as priests, or even, necessarily, as people of superior intelligence and feeling. Though I'm sure I once did, and once in a while still do. What Auden and J. V. Cunningham have believed before me is probably nearest the truth: that the poet's real, and perhaps only, magic is with words. He begins his life with a natural gift for handling them and for hearing them. He loves them for their sounds, their tastes, their soft or steel feel. And for their enduring strangeness. When he is young, they are among his most pleasurable and reliable toys. He enjoys them.

Joyce records, perhaps more graphically than anyone else, this early sort of pleasure. Stephen Dadaelus is in his first year at Clongowes Wood School, when he hears one of his schoolmates call another a "suck."

Suck was a queer word. The fellow called Simon
Moonan that name because Simon Moonan use
to tie the prefect's false sleeves behind his back
and the prefect used to let on to be angry. But
the sound was ugly. Once he had washed his
hands in the lavatory of the Wicklow Hotel and
his father pulled the stopper up by the chain
after and the dirty water went down through
the hole in the basin. And when it had all gone
down slowly the hole in the basin had made a
sound like that: suck. Only louder.

Like Stephen, the young poet recognizes that each word
has, for him, its own perfect story. Its own concrete significance is only the beginning.

The poet does something more with his natural gift;
he refines it. At first by play, later by work, he civilizes
it. He begins, perhaps not even consciously, by imitating
the styles of the great masters. When he is very young, he
may try on Shakespeare's cod-piece, the drugs of Cole-
ridge, Byron's love-life, the melancholia of Tennyson or
Poe. Later on he may discover Hopkins, Yeats, Robert
Lowell . . . . But Style is not simply a way of saying
things; it is a way of seeing things. And seeing them with
the whole being at once—not merely with the eye. Poetry
is felt thought, Eliot once said. And so it is. But being
both at once, it is neither. It is seeing, thinking, feeling all
at once with that *gestalt* which is the body-mind. A poem
is an experience of a total kind, a moment of existence.
So,—truly to imitate the masters is to try on their psyche
and their vision through the medium of language. It is
to stretch our own meager capacities. To enable us to
create new capacities in ourselves that our perceptions
may equal or surpass their own power to invent and to
perceive. It is to experience our world as they did—or
might, in order to experience it as they never could have.

As Ben Jonson pointed out in his little essay, *Timber,
or Discoveries,* "slavish imitation" is an undesirable condition for a poet. Eventually, he must cut loose from his

models and move into his own design. And so, at last, if he is really good, he begins to invent. The development of my own work follows this pattern. From 1955 to 1964 I wrote and published poems in the manner of Yeats, of Lowell, and Roethke. Traditional poems in traditional meters and rhyme schemes.

". . . animals and children *make* faces," says W. H. Auden, "but they do not have one." And there is the old Zen *Koan* which asks, "What was your face before you were born?"

The mature poet's task is to create his face, to have one. So, in 1965, I began to throw out all the traditional rhetoric I had learned in nine years. I began to write in syllabics or accentual meter; often I picked deliberately "unpoetic" subjects. It's easy to write a poem about the death of someone you love, but how about one on weeds or the healthy old man next door picking his tomatoes? At the same time, I began to experiment in a direction quite familiar to the classical oriental poets and the early imagists. How much of an experience could you omit,— how much language could you cut away—and still have a poem? Formerly, like most poets of the Fifties, I had made poems by accumulation, by adding one thing to another, thought to thought, image to image. Now, I began like a sculptor to work by subtraction; to start with a large, raw block and to chisel away all but the absolutely essential. Adjectives and adverbs withered away in wholesale lots, and poems were stripped down to nouns and verbs. Often 20 or 30 words proved not only enough, but the maximum. Any more and the pieces suffered a lesion of tension. By this time, of course, I was in danger of writing the perfect poem—the blank page.

I have now, long since, begun putting things back into my poems, though not in the manner of my earlier work. My lines, though having no set length, have once again become metrical. And there has been a corresponding change in the aesthetic governing the poems. Whereas, in my earlier work, the emphasis had been on capturing the text of an experience or an object as it actually was, along with an exact emotional tenor; in my more recent work, the tendency is to treat both the real and the imagined as having, as in fact they do, the same intellectual and emotional validity and integrity. Correspondingly, there is less of a pre-conceived plan for each poem and more reliance on the intrinsic demands of the basic material of the poem and on the luck of the unconscious.

Now—what does the midwest have to do with all this, since it is where I have lived and worked for nearly 20 years? One might naturally suppose a relationship, but is there really more than a superficial one?

Where one comes out on this question is at least partly determined by how one understands the term, "Midwest." Is it more than a geographic term of location? I don't think so. This is the era of Mass-Cult. We have great mobility and nearly instantaneous communications. (Even if these communications mean, in actuality, imprecision and the swifter communication of falseness and inaccuracy.) This means that to be born in Whitewater is not necessarily to be reared there, and to be raised in New Orleans is not necessarily, or even probably, to remain there. It is a commonplace of our experience that many mid-westerners are not natives at all, but displaced Southerners or Easterners, and many New Yorkers are mid-westerners, etc. Secondly, the mini-skirt in Minneapolis is likely to be just as short as in London or Paris. And, finally, mobility and nearly instant verbal and visual communication, aside from eroding distinctly regional characteristics, have perhaps shown us simply that much of what we may once have thought were distinctly local characteristics are not after all local and unique. Take the supposedly regional poets Edwin Arlington Robinson and Edgar Lee Masters. Here's Masters' "Anne Rutledge":

Out of me unworthy and unknown
the vibrations of deathless music;
"With malice toward none, with charity for all."
Out of me the forgiveness of millions toward millions,
and the beneficent face of a nation
Shining with justice and truth.

I am Anne Rutledge who sleep beneath these weeds,
Beloved in life of Abraham Lincoln
Wedded to him, not through Union
But through separation.
Bloom forever, O Republic,
From the dust of my bosom!"

Here's Robinson's "Mr. Flood . . ."

Well, Mr. Flood, we have the harvest moon
Again, and we may not have any more;
The bird is on the wing, the poet says,
And you and I have said it here before.
Drink to the bird." He raised up to the light
The jug that he had gone so far to fill,
And answered huskily: 'Well, Mr. Flood,
Since you propose it, I believe I will.

There is little if anything to identify either of these poems
as particularly eastern or midwestern. Probably every
small town in America has its Eben Flood, and the op-
timism of Anne Rutledge sounds as much like Brooklyn's
Walt Whitman as anybody. Even the diction and rhythms
of these poems are not particularly regional; probably
Robert Frost alone of American poets has made consist-
ent currency of a local dialect.

Shall we talk of midwestern rural conservatism and
puritanism? I suspect we shall find it not much different
from that of New England. Shall we talk of pessimism and
the grotesque? I suspect the Snopeses reign in Chigger-
bank, Michigan, with the same *joie de vivre* they do in
Oxford, Mississippi. Shall we speak of idealism and op-
timism in Minot, North Dakota, and Carmel, California?
I suspect that the price of dune-buggies is only slightly
more than that of custom-made surfboards. Finally, we

might compare the problems of American higher education at Columbia and Harvard, Wisconsin and Chicago, UC at Berkeley and Stanford. Local characteristics and their influence today are minimal. Perhaps they have always been minimal, insistence on regionalism to the contrary. But these are ultimately questions for the sociologist of literature, I think, and not for the poet himself. For the poet, there is the *place* (and all the other places he has ever been or can imagine); there is its visual design, its auditory signature, its people. This is his material. It is not whether the birch tree is in Vermont, Michigan, or Oregon that is significant, but whether or not one is the swinger.

And now, having said all that, I want to enter a demurrer and postscript to my own argument. Place *may* be important to a poet and may establish him or help to establish him as part of a *trend*. But only if we understand trend to mean "the way things have been going for a long, long time." And only if we understand place as Hemingway understood Paris—as a "moveable feast."

Trends and places seem to me fraternal quadruplets. The older pair bear the names Urban and Rural; and the other pair, younger by a few minutes perhaps, the names Classical and Romantic. T. E. Hulme, in his essay on the subject, distinguished the classical by its preoccupation with society as a whole and with the individual only as a social entity. Its artistic characteristics are the establishment and perpetuation of the traditional in subject matter and style and its objectivity of point of view; i.e. that the poet does not identify with his hero, or to put it another way: he is not himself the focus of his own poem. Homer is not Achilles. Moliere is not Le Misanthrope. Swift is not Gulliver. Philosophically and scientifically, it means man sees the universe in terms of logical mechanics, and human nature is reducible to rational principles.

One can easily see the connection, I think, between the Classical point of view and Urban life. When men mass themselves in cities, they consciously or unconsciously yield up some of their freedom of action in exchange for the benefits of city culture. They submit to laws needed to regulate the flow of human traffic, and irrational acts are viewed with alarm and met by cries of "law and order." Man is less likely, in a city, to see himself as a hero or a god. And poetry arising out of such a matrix is likely to bear a freight mainly of social criticism. The aim of classical poetry, as Horace pointed out, is first to instruct. Satire may have been born among country Greeks, but it found its true home in the city: Athens, Rome, Paris, New York. Its focal point is usually the foolishness and irrationality of men; and its aim: to bring man to rational order. This, whether one is speaking of Juvenal and Lucan, Pope and Swift, or Kenneth Koch of the current New York School, so called. As a matter of fact, in Koch's poem, "Fresh Air," we even get a musty whiff of *The Dunciad*:

> A blond man stands up and says,
> "He is right! Why should we be organized to defend
>         the kingdom
> Of dullness? There are so many slimy people con-
>         nected with poetry,
> Too, and people who know nothing about it!
> I am not recommending that poets like each other
>         and organize to fight them,
> But simply that lightning strike them.

On the other hand, the Rural and Romantic are often complementary. It is not difficult to see how, isolated in Nature, both fighting her and dependent on her for survival, Man is likely to stress individual character and perception. Self-reliance, Individualism, and laissez-faire become the shibboleths by which he lives. In such a milieu, Man more easily sees himself as heroic; he may even achieve the legendary status accorded to minor and local deities. He becomes Prometheus or Moses, Crazy Horse or Johnny Appleseed. In the philosophical and scientific aspect, Romanticism more often than not means seeing the universe as mysterious in its workings and often irrational. Correspondingly, man is not reducible to a set of logical principles governing human nature; he is more often Mike Hammer (judge, jury, and executioner) than he is Philip Marlowe; Horatio Alger, Jay Gatsby, or Frankenstein, but seldom if ever Huckleberry Finn or Nick Carraway. In the art of poetry, Romanticism means principally two things: a tendency of the author to identify closely with the hero of the poem; or, as in the case of Blake, Keats, Whitman, and Yeats, often to become oneself the focus of the poem. And secondly, since the Romantic artist believes in his unique inventive capacities and the particularity of his own vision and experience of the world, he is likely to junk the past in its traditional and formal aspects, and to create his own shapes and cadences.

*Robert
Dana
73*

Now, there are, of course, exceptions to this simplified view. There are urban Romantics and rural Classicists. There are masters who mix, like a vodka martini, a classical technique with a romantic attitude toward their material; and there are those who, like Pound and Eliot, embody a classical perspective in a romantic style. But as I have outlined them, these are the main lines of development of Western literature since it began. And American poetry of the 1960's and 70's did not invent itself. The rise of the Fugitives at Vanderbilt in the 1920's marked the continuation and refinement of classical principles in American poetry. The line of continuation passes from John Crowe Ransome to early Robert Lowell to the poets anthologized in *New Poets of England and America*. Then, around 1956, the resurgence of American Romanticism from San Francisco, its genesis something like Whitman to Patchen-Williams to Ginsberg and Snyder and Creeley. (See Don Allen's *The New American Poetry*.) Then, a western resurgence of classicism led by Yvor

Winters, J. V. Cunningham, and Edgar Bowers. And now a third wave of American romanticism heralded by Paul Carroll's anthology *The Young American Poets.* More remarkable perhaps is the shift to freer technique and a more varied and chancy style by previously formal poets like Robert Lowell, James Wright, and even J. V. Cunningham.

So, where does my work stand in relation to all of this? Well, it was shaped by all these currents and cross-currents, one way or another, for better or worse. You may read it for yourself and decide the relationship. But as you make your judgment, it might be well to remember the Henry of John Berryman's 77 *Dream Songs*:

> *These* fierce & airy occupations, and love,
> raved away so many of Henry's year
> it is a wonder that, with in each hand
> one of his own mad books and all,
> ancient fires for eyes, his head full
> & his heart full, he's making ready to move on.

Selections From

A STILLNESS AT THE CENTER OF THE TARGET

*Robert*
:12                                                          *Dana*

We listened for it at the wind's back                        *75*
that darkness you can hear

It slips down
under trees leaved with fire and light
as if to a river's edge
sipping the waters like some familiar animal

In the bright vowels of three puddles
it remembers the bare stone

Now it seems important to ignore ourselves
to undress into our own flesh
to gather from the earth its sharp fires

It seems important
to make no move the snow will look back on

:13

*Robert Dana* 76

It has been evening all day
Midwinter rain sleek and raw

Nine days it has been falling on Los Angeles
Great trees gutter
Canyons with their houses slump into the sea

Now the trucks are made ready again
and the refugees take the darkness from their shoes
They hear grief hum in the heavy metal

Some are relieved to be carrying away nothing
Some bear letters of introduction some knives
None asks where
The trucks move out in the direction of the mountains

At first light
small birds cry in Syrian "Sirhan! Sirhan!"
and the wolf lies on the left side of his blood
slowing into sleep

Across the lake the capital swelters
Power sleeps in its brass crib                    *Robert*
like a beautiful child with nothing in her sleeves    *Dana*

The guardsmen have left                            77
taking with them the order of knives
The legislators have closed their teeth on the law and gone home

In the streets of the city
the young make a carnival in their clothes
They say 'We have died too often'
They say 'We have not lived'

One sits on the sidewalk trying the small flavors of desire
Another photographs the picture of a train
Others their eyes small stones
pass in twos and threes the many-figured doors
doors closed and locked
doors ajar
doors lit to cold rooms where the questions are kept

We are what has become of them
We sit here
It is night still to the bottom of the sky
Somewhere beyond our vision a boat is moving
Its waves argue with the soft beach
We have believed too little

I am the angler at the edge of darkness
You are morning in the orange garden of your dress
Here is the savage the simple

blind worth

man    woman    water returning    earth

:29

*Robert*
*Dana*
78

Grey day after day after grey day
unseasonable cold
and the rain moving toward him again

If he sleeps
it's like a burning building
If he dreams
it's of neither fire nor water

A door opens into the books of history's black fashion

*

This is love's blind corner
This is shadow

In the moonlight
the slick ponies carouse and are riderless
Where the dogs take the darkness in their teeth
lovers take their silence in their arms
and night turns
in the complexity of its disasters

But theirs are not more than they have made them
Nothing is simple

Between them
loneliness is what is left of the sacred
In the inner kiss of breath
the marriage
the laughter

*

When he wakes
the meadows of this dream are empty

But the air is alive still
at its own delicate ear
A dove feathered in blood
bursts from his forehead
and the sun is a deep bell
and is ringing

They had carried within themselves
all their lives their lives
They had been walking toward each other for years

Hopelessness is not one of the vows of marriage

Admitting evil
they forgive themselves nothing
They share their pain
Each that the other's may be less

The city rises below them like cakes of pure ice
or spills away like a shatter of jewels
If the iron ape hunches in the plaza
In the incredible cold
if the manhunt is on
the bomb ticking

Still from the great lake
the surf loops steadily toward the shore

It blesses them with its indifference

They will not lose tomorrow
nor the silver key in the ashtray
nor the sense of the door closing behind them
Though they will not find
the perfect rings they have been looking for

Along the winter park
it will not seem strange to them
that their madness warms
and casts its light across the snow

At the Aquarium
the fishes move in a suspended light

in their wet heavens
flow and touch

*Robert*
*Dana*
79

:40

Each day waits on the next
for the last

a fact to the body
like a memory of the future

To love you was nothing simple
but most of a life life was searching

What we had together
seemed altogether possible
Easy as the water our backs dipped into after sleep

You knew the magic children in your flesh
You liked eggs
You were afraid of doorbells

And I remember the irises of your eyes happy as cracked glass

But if I thought I knew you
it was just such a mistake as I'd made before
in a garden into which salt rained continually
This time in a blue canyon
and on the long highways

I am blind now with looking into it
so it doesn't matter

It doesn't matter
that winter spreads its bleak arts between us
that every spring flowers into a mind of colors

There's another way to begin

BIBLIOGRAPHY

BOOKS

1957 *My Glass Brother and other poems,* The Constance Press, now
   The Stonewall Press, Iowa City (limited edition, 50 copies)
1964 *The Dark Flags of Waking,* The Qara Press, Iowa City (limited edition, 500 copies)
1966 *Journeys From The Skin,* The Hundred Pound Press, Iowa
   City (limited edition, 250 copies)
1967 *Some Versions of Silence,* W. W. Norton, New York
1971 *The Power of the Visible,* The Swallow Press, Chicago

*Robert Dana 81*

POEMS

1955 "My Glass Brother," *Poetry,* March
1957 "For Sister Mary Apolline," *Poetry,* January
1959 "Between Seasons," *Frescoe,* Summer
1962 "Meditations on a Woman's Voice," *The Paris Review,* Fall
   "Words For My Wife," *The Sewanee Review,* Summer
1963 "Journeys From The Skin" (part I) (under the title "Life and
   Times. I"). *The Prairie Schooner,* Fall
1964 "A Winter's Tale," *The New Yorker,* February 7
   "A Plain Riddle," "Second Riddle," "Wild Raspberries,"
   "The Lovers," *The North American Review,* Summer
   "Some Versions of Silence," sections 1 and 2, *The North
   American Review,* Winter
1965 "Journeys From The Skin," (part II), *The Sewanee Review,*
   Winter
   "Five Riddles," *The Nation,* August 2
1966 "Pop: At Checkers," "Thoughts Before Sleep," *The West
   Coast Review* (Canada), Spring
   "Some Versions of Silence," sections 5, 6, 8, and 10, *Poetry,*
   May
1967 "The Man En Route," "Waiting," *The Northwest Review,*
   Fall
   "At Heinhold's Last Chance Bar," *San Francisco,* May
   "Picking It Up," *The North American Review,* September
1968 "Twelve Poems From The T'ang," (translations of Wang
   Wei, Li Po, Liu Ch'ang-ching, Liu Chung-yung, Tu Fu,
   Ssu-k'ung Shu, Li Shang-yin, and Wei Ying-wu), *Stony
   Brook Journal of Poetry,* 1/2
   "The Unbroken Code," *The New York Times,* April 15
   "Fever," *The New York Times,* May 6
   "Passage," *The Nation,* November 15
   "The Lie," "A Taste of Anise," *The North American Review,*
   Nov.-Dec.
1969 "A Poem Carved Verbatim . . .," *The West Coast Review,*
   (Canada), Spring

1970    "Merlin, At the End," "Anti-World," "If You Answer," *The West Coast Review* (Canada), Spring

"The Stillness at the Center of the Target," sections 21 and 22, *The Iowa Review*, 1/3

"The Stillness at the Center of the Target," sections 13 and 17, *The North American Review*, Winter.

"The Stillness at the Center of the Target," sections 3, 7, and 10, (under the title "The Woman on the Mall"), *The New Yorker*, November 21.

1971    "The Stillness at the Center of the Target," section 14 (under the title "The Winter and The Snow,") *The New Yorker*, January 16

1972    "Picking It Up," "The Stone Garden," "The Drunkard," "The Joy Tree," *The Quarterly Review of Literature*, Summer

"The Power of Governors," *Book*, April

"The Stillness at the Center of the Target," section 31 (under the title "Vision and Transformation," (*The New Yorker*, September 2

1973    "The Stillness at the Center of the Target," Section 39 (under the title "Christmas, 1972: The Gift of Fire," *The Nation*,

*Poems in Anthologies*

1957    "The Seaman's Prayer," *Homage to Baudelaire*, Cummington Press, Iowa City

1960    "Notes on a Child's Coloring Book," *Poetry for Pleasure*, Doubleday

1961    "Goodbye. Goodbye." *Midland*, Random House

1968    "On the Expressway," *On City Streets*, Evans-Lippincott, and Bantam

1969    "A Winter's Tale," *The New Yorker Book of Poems*, Viking

1970    "The Unbroken Code," *The New York Times Book of Verse*, Macmillan.

1973    "The Stillness at the Center of the Target," sections 34 and 35 (under the titles "Missing You" and "Love's Body" in *Letters*, The Wine Press, Chicago, (limited edition).

*Reviews of other Poets*

1961    "Four Odd and One Even," *The Prairie Schooner*, Spring

1962    "Dialogue in Limbo," *The Prairie Schooner*, Fall

"Double Martini & Broken Crankshaft," *The Prairie Schooner*, Winter

"Recent Poetry and The Small Press," *The North American Review*, Fall

1967    "Five Anthologies," *Poetry*, April

*Plays*

1967    "The Trunk," *The North American Review,* March

*Literary Criticism*

1970    "The Stutter of Eternity: A Study of the Themes of Isolation and Meaninglessness in Three Novels by Yukio Mishima," *Critique: Studies in Modern Fiction*

*Reviews*

*My Glass Brother and other poems* in "Twenty Three Poets" by Don Geiger, *Prairie Schooner,* xxxii, no. 3, Fall, 1958

*Some Versions of Silence* in *Library Journal,* vol. 92, April, 1967

──────────────in *Choice,* vol. 4, no. 12, February, 1968

──────────────by William Heyen, in *Poetry,* vol. III, February, 1968

*The Power of the Visible* in "Poems From Things Lost and Concealed," by Ralph J. Mills, Jr., Chicago *Sun-Times,* May 7, 1972

──────────────in "The Poetry Beat," by Ron Offen, Chicago *Daily News,* June 10, 1972

*Biographical Note:*

Robert Dana was born in Massachusetts, but he has lived much of his life in the Midwest. He has been on the faculty of Cornell College in Mt. Vernon, Iowa, since 1953, where he now holds the rank of Professor of English. He has been the recipient of a Rinehard Award and an AMC Ford Asian Studies grant at Berkeley, and he was Editor of *North American Review* from 1967 to 1969.

## COLOPHON

The pagination is by paper, not type, page, a bibliographical experiment. The Sebenthall section is printed on Linweave Text, the McGrath section on Linweave Super White, and the Dana section on Curtis Colophon, to help personalize each author. The type is Times New Roman, designed by Stanley Morison, set by La Crosse Composing. Sewing and casing are by Frank Nekola. 500 copies (50 signed) were designed and printed by Emerson G. Wulling, Sumac Press.